Becoming Your Child's

First and Most Important

Teacher

By

Robert P. Newberry

Raising Successful Children Series

Book Two

Library of Congress Cataloging-in-Publication Data on file with the Library of Congress

ISBN: 978-0-692-19894-0

Published in the United States by:

Green Beans Publishing
c/o Robert P. Newberry
PO Box 233
Munnsville, New York 13409

www.RobertPNewberry.com

Printed in the United States of America

Books are available in quantity for distribution to educators and counselors, for promotional or educational use. Write to Book Sales, Green Beans Publishing, c/o Robert Newberry, PO Box 233, Munnsville, New York, for information about discounts and terms or call 315.762.3877

Reviews of *Green Beans and Legacies (Book #1: Raising Successful Children Series)*

Excellent book, very easy to read and engaging. I enjoyed the personal touches and stories throughout the book. I will recommend this book to the parents I work with in my professional setting, as well as use it in my every day parenting of my children. B. Abbey

This is a MUST READ for anyone who interacts with children. As an elementary teacher for over 20 years, I can say that Green Beans and Legacies is the most influential book I've read in a long time. It is well written and full of personal and relevant reflections all parents can relate to. This book will become part of my library on loan to parents of my students. As a father, the lessons and stories in this book often helped me be a much better parent. C. Clarke

The book is a quick read, but one whose readers will consult regularly. It is entertaining, empowering, informative, and inspiring. A copy of this book should be placed in the hands of every parent and grandparent. I intend to share it with my son, daughter and granddaughter, knowing that they will be better parents for having read and followed the suggestions in this book. I highly recommend that you do likewise. M. Seagriff, author

No matter what stage of raising your children you are at, this book will provide the kind of guidance that is needed in such a journey. I have found other parenting and family focused books to be overwhelming. Robert Newberry gives a thoughtful perspective on how the difficult work of raising children can be rewarding and enjoyable. I simply loved every bit of it! A. Matthews

This book was a joy to read, and a "must have" for all parents, grandparents and anyone who has the privilege of influencing children, growing up. I think it should be mandatory reading for all parents of young children. F. Pisano

Dedicated to our three children:

Tara, Tim and Jesse and their spouses Bob, Casey and Chris. We are thrilled watching you become your children's first and most important teachers.

Preface:

For parents whose families are not intact

I know that family make-up is changing. If my grade school teacher in the early 1960's asked my classmates and me to raise our hands if our parents were separated or divorced, it is possible that my hand would have been one of only a few raised as my parents divorced when I was in elementary school. If that exercise were duplicated in one of today's classrooms, the majority of hands would be raised. The intact family is becoming rarer.

This is the second book in the *Raising Successful Children Series*. Successful children, for me, are children who become happy, productive, moral and purposeful adults. We often hear that children most often do best when raised in two parent families and the guidance offered in this book may seem to presume an intact family. Let's talk about that.

If the family that you lead is not intact, the focus of your parenting will need to be the same as if your family was intact. Your focus must remain on helping your child build a successful future. You might have to make some adjustments along the way and your task might be quite a bit more challenging, but whether your family is intact or not, you <u>can</u> raise your child to build a successful future.

For years, I have talked to many parents about their children, how they approach their parental responsibilities and the results they are getting. Many of those parents have been separated or divorced, and I have often shared with them my own divorced parents' examples. My brother and I were most fortunate that our parents were guided by what my brother and I needed, not by what might make them happy in the short term. Their happiness was secondary to ours. Here are two examples.

First, my brother and I lived with our mother, though we spent time with our father on weekends. I recall a particular evening when my brother and I were giving our mom a pretty rough time. I don't recall the specifics but do remember that I was in our bedroom refusing to come out. My brother opened our bedroom door and told me to come out and walk to the living room. I refused. He then told me that I had better move fast because our father was in the living room with our mother and wanted to speak with us. Surprise! Surprise! I immediately walked into the living room where my brother and I sat and listened to our divorced parents, together, read us the riot act and outline how they expected us to behave. This memory is over 50 years old, but it is as vivid today as it was then. I am sure that we listened quietly and followed their directives.

Second, my brother was in his final year of college and I was a new college student beginning my first year. That fall my brother and I received letters from our father telling us of his impending second marriage. Several weeks later, we received letters from our mother telling us of her impending second marriage. I recall laughing to myself about the letters thinking that once I moved out of the house all the changes started! What was very clear to my brother and me was that while our divorced parents may have desired to remarry earlier, they postponed doing so until both of us were well on our way to adulthood and out of the house. Their happiness was secondary to meeting the needs of us boys.

I've shared these and other stories with parents because, though our family was not intact, our parents handled their parenting responsibilities from the perspective of what their children needed. This guided their parenting, and I am forever grateful for their doing so.

But what about the parent who confronts the challenge of raising a child or children by him or herself? This has not been

8

my experience as child or parent. However, I am aware of numerous instances in which this very difficult task has been done successfully.

Dr. Ben Carson, world-renowned neurosurgeon and recent Presidential candidate, has recounted his experience of being one of two boys raised by a single parent. It is an inspiring, gut-wrenching story. I encourage you to learn about his courageous, tenacious mother. His story and many others that I have witnessed describe a profile of a single parent who:

- After initially feeling the unfairness of having to rear the child(ren) alone, embraces a dream of raising a child who goes onto build a successful future and,

- Demonstrates tremendous courage, tenacity and self-sacrifice in giving priority to being a parent attentive to the needs of his or her child.

I have often said to parents embracing this task that the absent parent will never have the joy of watching their child grow up. Nor will the absent parent experience the tremendous gift of receiving when that child is in his or her early to **mid-twenties** a call or visit to thank **the present parent** for all that has been done and sacrificed so that he or she could be well on the way to building a successful life. I usually finish such a conversation with, "Buckle up! You can be a successful parent, regardless of your circumstances. Your child needs you to be."

As I discuss family life, I am going to borrow the Search Institute's definition of a parenting adult: an adult who, regardless of their biological relationship, assumes responsibility for a child. The task of helping your child build a successful future is tremendously important, as you know. I appreciate the importance you place on your parenting as reflected in your taking the time to read this book.

The Parent as Teacher

Introduction

By way of introduction, I am a retired public-school counselor, having spent many years with many young people. I am also the father of three wonderful adult children and grandfather of ten! I **have been** married to Mary Jo for 45 years.

In addition to my public-school work, I have had the opportunity for many years to share my ideas about helping youth build successful lives with a wide range of people living in various parts of our country. Included among these opportunities are:

- Presenting at numerous national, state and regional conferences about children, achieving and adversity;

- Consulting with, developing and delivering programming for schools, military and community organizations that focus on helping young people excel regardless of challenges and circumstances they encounter;

- Communicating in a variety of formats (book, blog, newsletter, social media) with thousands of parents about raising successful children.

In recent years I have also become a Licensed Mental Health Counselor and currently work as a therapist in a mental health clinic.

For a long time, I have been very concerned about how children and families are doing. I speak with too many children who are not being prepared for or learning what it takes to build successful lives. I thought at first that I could make a contribution by sharing with parents what I have been teaching young people about building successful futures. Then I realized that what concerns me most is that a growing number of children do not look to their parents as a primary source of guidance and direction. Many children are choosing to be influenced by aspects of the culture other than their parents.

So, I reconsidered my plan of attack and went back to the fundamentals. I reasoned that the outcome of successful parenting is a child who becomes a happy, purposeful, moral and responsible adult. This is the end that parents should have in mind as they raise their children. Next, for a parent to accomplish this outcome, it is vital that the child learns to embrace two key concepts:

> ▪ First, the child must develop a DESIRE TO GROW AND MATURE, to become his or her best. The child must develop an internal hunger to aspire, stretch and build a positive future.

> ▪ Second, the child must also acquire a DISPOSITION TO LEARN, recognizing and accepting the value of learning the important lessons of life from his or her parents.

Finally, a family culture that can nurture and help a child to learn about and embrace these two concepts — a *desire to grow and mature* and a *disposition to learn* from his or her parents--is all important. You have the capacity to create such an affirming family culture. Doing so is rooted in you being your child's first and most important teacher. When this occurs, the likelihood of your child becoming a happy, purposeful, moral and responsible adult is greatly enhanced.

The purpose of this book is to help you to build such a family culture, enabling you to become your child's first and most important teacher.

Two Key Behavior Patterns

A Desire to Grow and Mature

As I watched a newly-born grandchild, it became clear very quickly that this child was highly motivated! When hungry, the baby enthusiastically made his or her desires known until they were addressed. "Feed me!" When uncomfortable, the child energetically addressed this need as well. "Change me!" Children are born with desire and motivation. These are not aspects of a child's make-up that need to be created. They do, however, need to be nurtured, directed and challenged.

I think of a young pre-school child I knew who had difficulty saying certain sounds which impacted his ability to speak and be understood. He was provided special instruction and practiced over and over. As he worked to improve, he was corrected numerous times, but he persisted. He became a very articulate and easily understood young man.

I recall a young person who picked up a basketball on a snowy, cold winter day and headed outdoors. She shoveled the driveway to allow for play in front of the basket and, despite the cold, shot and shot and shot. Her skill level improved, and she became very successful in her basketball league.

Noted educator, Jaime Escalante, is portrayed in the movie, *Stand and Deliver*, imploring his inner city, Latino students about having *ganas*, an internal desire to excel and become his or her best.

A *Desire to Grow* is not about desire alone. That is already present. Helping your child acquire a *Desire to Grow* involves helping your child develop a desire to become his or her best person, including:

- developing unique talents and abilities,

- interacting positively with peers and adults, and

- being a giving and loving family member.

This *Desire to Grow* that I am describing does *not* involve your child behaving in these ways in order to seek approval or avoid punishments and being ostracized. Perhaps in your child's early years, these reasons may suffice. Long term, they are not adequate because the significant adults in your child's life will not always be present. Your child needs to personally embrace a desire to grow and pursue his or her best independently. A *Desire to Grow* is a mature and responsible hunger to do what is right and worthy because doing so is right and worthy.

A Disposition to Learn

I remember my older brother arriving home from school and telling me he had something to show me. He had learned how to do a "bounce pass" with a basketball that day in gym class and wanted to teach me how to do it. I ran with him to the barn which served as our basketball court and listened to his instruction. I worked to duplicate what he was telling and showing me, over and over. Finally, I mastered how to bounce pass a basketball!

I also remember returning home from my first year of college and being invited by my father to go to his favorite restaurant for dinner. As we drove to the restaurant we were discussing something about which, as a new college student, I was emphatically sharing my new-found insights and "wisdom." I forget the topic about which we were talking but I remember sharing an opinion that was very much at odds with my father's.

13

I also recall that my style was not one of discussing but rather dictating. With all of my newly acquired knowledge, I was likely pretty obnoxious. My father, finally tired of my arrogance and ignorance, interrupted me. He told me, "I want you to remember something, Bob. I know more than you do." I immediately went silent. Moisture started to accumulate in my eyes. Over 40 years ago, my father had in two short sentences reminded me of an important fact that I had forgotten. That fact was true then and remained true as long as he lived.

A *Disposition To Learn* is rooted in your child's desire to become his or her best. With this perspective, your child will value the knowledge, insights and wisdom possessed by the significant people in his or her life. In order to learn what these significant people have to offer, your child will see the importance of assuming the role of student and being coachable.

Most Important Teacher

Becoming your child's most important teacher is no easy task. Compared to parents of only a few years ago, today's parents are competing with a greater variety of factors in seeking to be the primary influence in the lives of their children. Whereas parents and churches were the two most significant influences in a child's life in the mid-20th century, today those two institutions compete with increasingly formidable factors such as 'the culture', media and peers.

Regardless of what the trend line is for which factors influence children most, what remains constant is a child's need for his or her parents to be a primary and significant positive influence.

When you are your child's most important and positive influence, he or she experiences:

- a vital positive, nurturing bond with you;

- affirmation and an unconditional commitment to his or her well-being regardless of your child's strengths, weaknesses, successes or

14

failures;

- appropriate and effective guidance and direction; and

- consistency and predictability on a daily basis. Your child can count on you.

All of these are vital elements of your child successfully developing into a happy, purposeful, moral and responsible adult. As you probably know, they are not always easily provided.

You've heard the phrase, I am sure, that "it takes a village to raise a child." My sense for the history of this phrase harkens back to a time when children were members of large, extended families which are tremendously positive familial structures within which to raise healthy children. Today, as families have become more nuclear and fractured, my sense is that this phrase represents the thinking that in light of the growing difficulties faced by today's parents in raising their children, the community should and can step up to compliment and in some instances take the place of the parent. It is important to maintain a proper perspective about the community, what it can do and what it cannot do.

However well-intentioned community efforts might be, such efforts fall short in filling the void that is created by unsuccessful parenting. Under the best of situations, community efforts are conditional, optional and inconsistent. Further, in advocating that community efforts can fill the void, a subtle message is sent to parents that raising children today is just too difficult a task. Rather than challenging parents to rise to meet the demands of being a successful parent, this approach provides a backdoor that accepts parental rationalizations and excuses. Mediocre parenting is accepted at the expense of exceptional and successful parenting. While it is true that much that goes on in our communities to support young people is worthy and admirable, *there is simply no replacement for responsible and effective parents.*

So, in spite of the challenges, it is vital that you embrace and be committed to being a successful parent! Your child needs and wants you to! Doing so will not be easy. Be assured, though you will likely feel from time to time that you are swimming against the current, you can be successful! This book will provide you with guidance on how to create a family culture that nurtures your child's hunger and desire to be his or her best as well as a disposition to learn the important lessons of life from you.

Two Transitions

Two important transitions take place when you successfully parent your child. First, he or she moves from being a dependent infant to becoming a happy, responsible, moral and purposeful adult.

The second transition that takes place involves you. Your role and duties will evolve. You will begin as your child's nurturer and teacher, albeit within the context of effectively exercising your parental authority. You will end up becoming a friend and coach to your adult child. What a thrill it will be to see your child do well as he or she successfully moves through this process into adulthood. Few experiences rival the enjoyment you will derive from your friendship with your adult child.

These two transitions will not just happen, however. *The fulcrum upon which you and your child make these two transitions is your effective use of your parental authority.* I find that it is this question of parental authority that parents struggle with most.

In the following pages, you will be asked to consider how you use your parental authority and the results you are getting from your parenting. You will be provided with different approaches to this question of parental authority, some unsuccessful and some very successful. You will be provided with effective guidelines that will enable you to significantly strengthen your positive influence in your child's life.

Live the View

The View

Sometime ago we visited Seattle, Washington and enjoyed zooming up to the top of the Space Needle. Rotating hourly, it offers a panoramic view of an absolutely beautiful part of the world. Slowly we turned and looked out over the city of Seattle and the various waterways and mountains of the Pacific Northwest.

Sitting at a table in the restaurant there, we were served by a waiter who placed drink coasters on the table before us. On each of the coasters was the phrase, "Live the View." Of course, the coasters were referring to the magnificent view of the Pacific Northwest. But, it occurred to me that the phrase also describes us. We do 'live the view' — our view. Our perspectives, attitudes and values comprise our 'view' and certainly affect how we act…and how we parent.

Parenting Styles According to Baumrind

The manner in which you parent can also be described as your style of parenting. It is a reflection of how you "view" the task of parenting. An extensive body of research about different parenting styles discusses this and is worth reviewing. Prominent parenting expert Diane Baumrind (1967) identified four very important aspects of your parenting. (See acknowledgments at the end of the book.) Together, they comprise your *parenting style*. They are:

- What disciplinary strategies do you use?

- Do you demonstrate warmth and nurturance towards your child and if so, how do you do it? (Parental Responsiveness)

18

- What communication styles do you use with your child?

- What are your expectations about maturity and self-control for your child? (Parental Demandingness)

Most parents have opinions about how "to do" each of these aspects of parenting. I'm sure you do. Consider why you handle each in the manner that you do. Your attitude or perspective--your view--about these aspects of parenting and how you "do" them, comprise your *Parenting Style*. **With this in mind, Baumrind identified several different parenting styles.** They are:

- Permissive/Indulgent

- Authoritarian/Dictatorial

- Authoritative (please note that this is different from Authoritarian/Dictatorial

A fourth has been added for our discussion here:

- Negligent/Disengaged

The Match Game

To identify your present parenting style, consider this scenario:

You have just received a phone call from a school principal telling you that your middle school-aged child and several classmates have been misbehaving in class. The students did not respond to continuous requests to cease and desist and were removed from their classroom. Due to their continued disrespectful behavior, the students, including your child, have been suspended from school for one day.

How would you respond and exercise your parental responsibilities and authority in such a scenario? Following are several possible parental responses. I have witnessed each one of them multiple times. Each one represents one of the four Parenting Styles cited above. After reviewing the various unlabeled parental responses, try to match each response to the Parenting Style it relates to most. Good luck!

Parental Response #1:

You listen to the school administrator. You explain to the principal that your child will never behave like this again. You state, furthermore, that you are the only one who will discipline your child. When your child arrives home, you yell and threaten your child. You scream, "Never will you behave that way again. You embarrass me when I get a call from the principal. Go to your room for the rest of the night!" You don't see your child until the next morning and don't talk about the preceding day's event. As your child leaves the house to board the approaching school bus, you yell at him, "Don't embarrass me today!!"

Parental Response #2:

Your initial response to the school administrator is to defend your child saying, "I don't believe that my child could ever behave as you have described. He (or she) never acts that way at home. Those other children are always causing trouble and that teacher has it in for my child. What are you going to do about them?" You maintain this perspective and when you meet with your child, you berate the school personnel for ganging up on him (or her). Further you encourage your child to stand up for him (or herself) in the future.

Parental Response #3:

You listen to the school administrator. You ask if it is possible for you and your child to meet with the principal and teacher as soon as possible. In addition to yourself, you want your child to hear from the educators themselves exactly what their concerns are and the rationale for the suspension. You also want your child to clearly understand that you are supportive of the educators' efforts and place a high priority on your child being successful at school.

After the meeting, you and your child return home. You invite your child to offer any reasons for the unacceptable behavior and discuss the importance of school performance. While discussing all of this, you make it clear that you support the educators' expectations. Further, you expect your child to behave and do his or her best in school because doing so is vital for a positive future. You outline for your child the loss of several privileges for the next several weeks due to the school situation and you explain that when he or she demonstrates responsible behavior at school, those suspended privileges will be restored.

Parental Response #4:

You see that the caller ID on your phone indicates a call from your child's school. You refuse to pick up the call and then when you see the call has terminated, you take the phone off the hook preventing future calls from coming through.

After reviewing the four parental responses, try to match each response to the related *Parenting Style* even though you have not been given descriptions of the four Parenting Styles. Good luck!

Parenting Style	Scenario Response
Permissive/Indulgent	?
Authoritarian/Dictatorial	?
Authoritative	?
Negligent/Disengaged	?

Answers are on the following page.

Answers to the *Match Game:*

Parenting Style	Scenario Response
Permissive/Indulgent	*2*
Authoritarian/Dictatorial	*1*
Authoritative	*3*
Negligent/Disengaged	*4*

The scenario cited in **The Match Game** is similar to so many I have seen through the years. The parental responses that were described are very realistic as well. Isn't it amazing that the same scenario can elicit such very different parental responses? How do you explain this? My explanation takes me back to the restaurant in Seattle. We really do live our 'views'. Because our 'views' are sometimes different, our parental responses will be different as well.

Did you identify the parental response and corresponding parental style which most closely resemble your own? Do you think one parenting style is more effective than another? Or, is the parenting style used by someone simply a reflection of that parent's disposition and not important?

I am reminded of one of my cooking adventures early in our marriage. My job was to prepare oatmeal for our breakfast. I followed the recipe on the box perfectly! When the oatmeal was done, I spooned it into our two bowls. My wife was the first to taste my creation. A pained look came across her face and I realized that something was wrong. Upon further examination, I realized that instead of 1/4 teaspoon of salt, I had placed 1/4 cup of salt into the oatmeal. You can imagine the resulting taste!

The ingredients in a recipe certainly affect the cooking results. Similarly, different parenting styles have different outcomes.

The parenting style you choose to use matters a great deal because, again, different parenting styles have different outcomes!

Parenting Styles Broken Down

Following are in depth descriptions of the Parenting Styles that have only been highlighted so far. Again, Baumrind is our primary resource here. (See acknowledgments at the end of the book.) Once a parent becomes aware of the various Parenting Styles and their typical outcomes, certain statements and points of view are no longer viable. No longer will comments such as "That's the way I was parented," or "That's just the way I am," be acceptable explanations for why a parent parents as he or she does. We have laughed about my placing too much salt in the oatmeal recipe many times over the years. But, if once I became aware of my error I continued to place too much salt in the oatmeal, it would stop being funny pretty quickly. *Awareness brings choice and choice brings the opportunity to improve and get better. With awareness, how you parent, the parenting style you use and the results you get, become a matter of your choice and intent.*

The Permissive or Indulgent Parenting Style

The Permissive or Indulgent Parenting Style (Parental Response #2) describes, from my observations, a growing number of today's parents. Parents who embrace this style care very much about their children. They are typically very responsive to their children's emotions but expect and demand very little of them. These parents consciously exert little or no control over their children. They establish few rules and those rules that are instituted are enforced very inconsistently.

Permissive Parents avoid routines because they want their children to feel unencumbered by such expectations. These parents are typically very accepting of the many ways that their children behave and avoid establishing any clear behavior boundaries or expectations. They often try to reason with and, if not successful, subtly manipulate their children to get them to behave. Rarely do they exercise their parental authority to influence their children's behavior. A Permissive Parent wants to avoid disciplining his or her child at all costs. Disciplining, reasons this parent, might threaten the parent-child relationship. The Permissive Parent aspires to be his or her child's friend, even during childhood.

Because Permissive Parents usually give their children what they want, these children learn to expect other adults such as neighbors, relatives and teachers to do the same. Children raised in this way typically become impulsive and reckless as they grow older. They demonstrate poor self-control. Permissive Parents often give their children numerous choices and options before their children's level of maturity allows them to choose wisely. *Children are forced to exercise choice before they are able to do so responsibly.* Because their parents do not make clear what acceptable or unacceptable behavior is, these children make many poor choices.

This lack of guidance and direction often results in children becoming rebellious and defiant. These children are more concerned with testing and challenging the limits of the structure within which they are operating, e.g. home, school, team and employment, than being purposeful and positively directed. They often demonstrate a lack of persistence in difficult or challenging situations and they are typically not receptive to guidance and advice from adults such as parents, teachers and coaches.

Helicopter Parents

We have already observed that Permissive Parents care deeply for their children. They are very responsive to the emotional concerns of their children. However, being responsive does not guarantee being helpful, effective or successful. Consider the example of Helicopter Parents.

Parents who use the Permissive Parenting Style work diligently to help their children avoid experiences that can be disappointing, frustrating or discouraging. Such experiences are not seen as opportunities for their children to acquire wisdom, maturity and insight. They reason that if these experiences can't be avoided entirely their unpleasant aspects need to be interrupted and minimized.

Working to protect their children from such difficult experiences, these parents become overly involved. From Little League to school or any other setting, they "hover", trying to protect their children. Hence, the label of 'Helicopter Parent' is born. The "children" being protected by today's helicopter parents range from elementary school students up through and including young adults in college and the work place! Sadly, while motivated to be helpful, helicopter parents are communicating to their child, "You don't have the ability to handle difficult situations." While wanting the best for their child, these parents are undermining the child's capacity to develop resilience and the skills necessary to successfully handle the inevitable challenges of life.

The concept of 'Helicopter Parent' has been joined by the 'Snow Plow Parent' who clears his or her child's way of any potentially adverse and challenging obstacles that might obstruct the child's progress. You can see that such activity is likened to a snow plow clearing the road of snow which makes traveling easier. Whether it is a helicopter or snow plow, the parental focus is not on raising and developing the child. The parental focus is on helping the child avoid inevitable challenges which are really opportunities that can be used for growth.

Summary

Permissive or Indulgent Parents want so much to build a strong bond and friendship with their children. *For all of the reasons cited above, this parenting style will **not** allow them to accomplish this.* Suffice it to say that as a child is growing up, he or she needs a parent to parent and not to be a friend. A parent should not begin to think about relating with his or her child as a friend until that child is in his or her early-mid 20's.

You can identify the Permissive Parenting Style when you hear a parent repeatedly using phrases such as these:

- "But what will my child think if I punish her?"

- "You can't do that to my child. I'll talk with him. He'll understand."

- "I want to be my child's friend as he grows up. He needs someone to talk with. I never had that."

- "Why are you doing this to my child?"

Consider how this parenting style addresses the four aspects of parenting highlighted earlier by Baumrind: Disciplinary Strategies, Warmth and Nurturance, Communication Styles and Expectations of a Child's Maturity and Self Control. Experience and research conclude that the Permissive/Indulgent Parenting Style is not effective in raising successful children

The Authoritarian or Dictatorial Parenting Style

Parents who use the Authoritarian or Dictatorial Parenting Style (Parental Response #1) are very demanding of their children, but not particularly responsive to their needs. In being demanding, these parents are primarily concerned about exerting control over their children and establishing strict rules without a rationale or explanation. These parents have little concern for preparing their children for the future as they make no effort to teach by explaining a purpose for their expectations or rules. Children are typically not provided with choices or options which provide opportunities for learning. Definitely, "my way or the highway" is the guiding principle in these households.

Parents who subscribe to this 'view' or style are typically very critical towards their children and do not display much warmth or affection. Their focus is primarily on their child's poor behavior and shortcomings. A child's violation of rules is an opportunity for scolding and punishment, not discipline and teaching. Parental concern, again, is about exercising control and authority, not effectively preparing the child for his or her future.

Summary

You will recognize the Authoritarian/Dictatorial Parenting Style when you hear a parent *repeatedly* make comments such as:

- "I'm the boss, period!"

- "I don't have to explain why. Just do it."

- "If you don't do it, I will knock you into next week!"

The volume is often on high as these statements are uttered.

What kind of results do parents get who embrace this parenting style? Children raised by Authoritarian/Dictatorial parents are typically obedient, but for the short term, and only when in the presence of the authority figure. They rank lower in happiness, self-esteem and how they interact with peers and adults. These children are described as anxious and withdrawn and react poorly to frustration. Girls raised by dictatorial parents are more likely to give up in challenging and frustrating situations while similarly raised boys typically demonstrate hostility in such circumstances.

The Disengaged or Neglectful Parenting Style

Originally, I was not going to comment about this parenting style. It likely does not relate to those who are reading this book because, by definition you are engaged and attentive to your child. But, I opted to include some brief observations in order to offer a broader perspective and continue to fill in the parenting styles frame of reference.

The Disengaged or Neglectful Parenting Style is best described as neither demanding nor responsive. This is evidenced in Parental Response #4. Prompted by an absence of concern, parents who embrace this parenting style will let their children behave with few if any guidelines. These parents convey little affection, warmth or involvement in their children's lives.

Children raised by parents who embrace this style sometimes force themselves to become independent because they cannot depend on their parents. More often, these children have great difficulty developing positive futures.

Conclusion

None of the parenting styles presented so far will allow you to realize your goal of successfully helping your child develop into a happy, purposeful, moral and responsible adult. On the chance that a child whose parent demonstrates any of these parenting styles builds a successful life, that success will be in spite of and not because of his or her parent.

Reflection Questions:

1. Do you see yourself in any of the 'views' or Parenting Styles described so far?

2. Are you pleased with how you are parenting or are some adjustments in order?

The Authoritative Parenting Style

Hey Momma, not to be self-righteous, but thank you for raising me to be respectful and courteous of others and everything else that u and dad passed onto me. I think you guys did a great job and I hope that I can do the same when I'm a parent. Love you!

A parent received this brief email message from a son who had just graduated from college and was launching into adulthood. This young man's parents are great examples of the Authoritative Parenting Style, not to be confused with the Authoritarian/Dictatorial Parenting Style. It is not unusual for an Authoritative Parent to hear this kind of message from his or her adult child. Following is another message received by two other Authoritative Parents.

Dear Mom and Dad,

Happy 35ᵗʰ anniversary. Doesn't seem like that long to me, but maybe that's because I've only been around for 28 of those years. I just wanted to thank you both for the life that you've given me and allowed me to have. I know that I can never say it enough, but I love you both. You've made me the person that I am today. Everything I've learned has a direct relation to the way you've chosen to live your lives, and how important you made me and my brother and our maturation. Everything I know about loyalty, respect and love, I've learned from the two of you. All of my successes, whether it be in school or at work, or in love, are directly related to the two of you. I've been really really lucky to have been blessed to have the two of you as my parents. All of the great things you have coming to you, you've more than earned over the years. If I could afford to send the two of you to Europe I would. Maybe someday. I hope you have a great day. Take yourselves out to dinner.

Parents who embrace this parenting style are effective at raising successful children. They do so by becoming their child's first and most important teacher.

Do you remember Parental Response #3 from **The Match Game** you played earlier? If you recall, this is one of four parental responses to a school situation involving a misbehaving child. Here it is again.

You listen to the school administrator. You ask if it is possible for you and your child to meet with the principal and teacher as soon as possible. In addition to yourself, you want your child to hear from the educators exactly what their concerns are and the rationale for the suspension. You also want your child to clearly understand that you are supportive of the educators' efforts and place a high priority on your child being successful at school. After the meeting, you and your child return home. You invite your child to offer any reasons for the unacceptable behavior and discuss the importance of school performance. While discussing all of this, you make it clear that you and the educators are on the same team. Further, you expect your child to behave and do his or her best because doing so is vital for a positive future. You also outline for your child the loss of several privileges for the next several weeks due to the school situation. You explain that when he or she demonstrates responsible behavior at school, those suspended privileges will be restored.

This is an example of the Authoritative Parenting Style in which parental authority is effectively used. In this response, the parent's concern was not simply to handle the immediate situation. The parent also wanted to ensure that his or her child would learn what acceptable and safe behavior is and to accept being accountable to people in positions of authority and responsibility.

Authoritative parents expect a lot from their children. They are also very concerned about their emotional well-being. Building warm and nurturing relationships with their children is important to them. A primary way that this concern is demonstrated is by establishing and enforcing rules and guidelines that their children are expected to follow. Parental enforcement of these expectations is done in a supportive and matter of fact way. Enforcement, appropriate teaching and encouragement about the importance of behaving are done by these parents in a manner that maintains parental expectations and enhances the child's emotional well-being. They understand correctly that these parental goals are complementary and not at odds with each other. Children who are raised by parents using this parenting style are typically positively motivated and confident. They interact well with peers and adults and demonstrate lower levels of problem behavior.

Utilizing the Authoritative Parenting Style allows you to meet many of your child's developmental needs. Creating a predictable and stable environment within which your child learns the ground rules that are required in order to grow and thrive, helps you to develop a positive and nurturing relationship with your child. You establish *credibility* in your child's eyes which allows you to serve as his or her teacher and guide, now and in the future. Your child learns to *respect* you and values your guidance.

Parental Credibility and Respect

Many of today's parents are confused about two vital concepts: *Credibility* and *Respect*. How does a parent gain parental credibility and respect from his or her child? The answer to this question is crucial because it is at the heart of a parent's ability to teach and influence his or her child. The different parenting styles offer different answers to this question.

I define *respect* as being admired, valued and held in high esteem. *Credibility*, I define as being believable, reliable and trustworthy. You need to be valued by your child and considered to be trustworthy in order to teach and influence him or her. When your child does not respect you, your guidance is not valued. When you lack credibility with your child, he or she considers you not to be trustworthy. Lacking both, your advice and direction will not be acknowledged or followed. This lack of credibility and respect prevents you from positively influencing your child going forward.

Parents who use the Authoritarian/Dictatorial Parenting Style think that credibility and respect automatically come with the title of 'Parent' and do not have to be earned. This parenting style expects that the child should comply blindly with the parent's wishes and orders. This may work in the very short term to get compliant behavior from a young and small child. It is important to understand, however, that the child's compliance is temporary at best and only due to the physical prowess of the parent and the young child's fear. It has no long-term usefulness.

Parents who use the Permissive/Indulgent Parenting Style think that credibility and respect result from being a 'friend' to their children. These parents are constantly placating their children, seeking their approval on numerous matters. The *Permissive* Parent opts not to administer discipline because he or she thinks that doing so may threaten the parent-child relationship.

Neither the Authoritarian/Dictatorial or Permissive/Indulgent parent builds credibility with his or her child. Parents who use these two parenting styles will find that their ability to teach and influence their children diminishes significantly as their children grow older. Parental credibility and respect are eroded, not enhanced over time, when using these Parenting Styles.

Credibility and respect are earned as you create a family culture that nurtures your child's disposition to learn and a desire to be his or her best. Without credibility and respect-seen through your child's eyes-you are talking to the wind and are mistaken when you think you are influencing your child's attitudes and behaviors.

When Hall of Fame football coach Vince Lombardi first assembled his Green Bay Packers football team after the team had experienced many losing seasons, he held up a football and said, "Gentlemen, this is a football." Starting with the basics, he created a franchise and a coaching legacy synonymous with excellence and success.

Because of the parental confusion I find regarding how to build a family culture that provides for parental credibility and respect, I developed a series of concrete and specific guidelines. Numerous parents have found them helpful. I call them **The Basics** and they reflect the "View" that is best represented by the Authoritative Parenting style. Utilizing **The Basics** will guide you as you help your child:

- Develop a desire to grow, mature and aspire to do what is right and worthy because doing so is right and worthy; and

- Develop a disposition to learn from you: his or her first and most important teacher.

Utilizing **The Basics** will help you:

- Facilitate two important transitions as your child moves from dependence to independence

and you move from being a parent to a
growing child within the context of authority,
to being a parent who is also friend and coach
to your adult child; and

- Earn credibility and respect from your child
allowing you to successfully help and teach
your child to be happy, productive, moral and
purposeful.

You will notice that **The Basics** do not offer a lot of how-to's or skills. More importantly, **The Basics** address your perspective and outlook about parenting and raising your child. Regardless of the stresses that you encounter in your life, e.g. work, finances etc., **The Basics** highlight what is important in raising your child from the perspective of your child's needs. When your "View" is right, the how to's and skills will come easily!!

I have chosen to make each of the three books in the **Raising Successful Children Series** reader-friendly. Doing so has allowed a wide range of people to find *Book One: Green Beans and Legacies*, helpful. This includes the single parent who struggled to achieve a GED as an alternative to a high school diploma, a parent with multiple college degrees and a grandparent who has numerous years of raising children under her belt.

Being reader-friendly does not diminish the validity or value of **The Basics**. In recent years, I have spent a great deal of time developing expertise in the clinical mental health field. It has been tremendous to be exposed to current, updated and cutting edge thinking and research in this area regarding children. In particular, I have focused this past year on current knowledge and insights from a variety of disciplines about brain development for both healthy and traumatized children. Since all functions and activities of a child are mediated by that child's brain, this work provides tremendous insight into how to raise healthy, happy and productive children. *What I have learned* *makes me even more enthusiastic and confident in sharing with you The Basics about raising successful children.*

The Basics

The Basics

1.   The responsibility of raising a child lies squarely on the parent's shoulders.

2.   A child earns privileges by successfully assuming responsibilities.

3.   A parent's example serves as a very influential model for a child to follow.

4.   A consistent, predictable environment allows a child to better understand the predictable structure of adult life.

5.   A parent's dreams for his or her child's future are very influential in the child's life.

6.   A lot of quality time is required to raise a successful child.

7.   A child's dignity and intrinsic value are derived largely from his or her relationship with the parent(s).

8.   Teaching a child a faith-based orientation to life is vital.

9.   A primary task for a parent is taking the mystery out of how to build a successful life for the child.

Basic #1

The responsibility of raising a child lies squarely on the parent's shoulders

A school teacher received a phone call one evening from one of his student's parents. Due to the child's poor report card, asked the parent, would the teacher threaten his child with various punishments because the child was just not doing his school work?

Eating lunch in a local pizzeria with one week of summer vacation remaining before school re-opens, a young child was misbehaving for her parent. The parent's friend commented, "Your child will be different next week once her teacher straightens her out."

I expect that the child whose father phoned the teacher and the child who misbehaved in the pizzeria, both benefit from their school structure and programs. However, if their parents continue to defer totally to other adults for solving these kinds of concerns, both children and parents will lose something very significant.

Our three children benefited tremendously from countless neighbors, teachers, coaches, pastors, aunts and uncles. Their contributions to our children were priceless and we are forever indebted to them. In each instance, however, their contributions were optional. Whenever things got a little difficult, these adults were not obligated to maintain their relationships with our children. A few examples include:

> ▪ An outstanding school principal with whom our son had bonded, leaving our area for career advancement.

- The wonderful coach with whom our daughter had a great relationship, had a disagreement with a school administrator and opted not to continue coaching our daughter's softball team.

- The wonderful aunt and uncle who retired and began spending half of their year in a warmer climate.

When my wife, Mary Jo, expects me to take care of the dirty dishes after a meal and I expect her to take care of them, the dishes do not typically get washed. When getting the job done is optional, each of us usually hopes or expects that the other will do the job. The dishes only get washed when one of us specifically takes on the responsibility of washing them.

When your child is growing up and you expect someone else to handle all or part of the task of raising him or her, your child will not be well served. He or she will lose out on a significant part of a developing relationship with you. Besides you, everyone's help, no matter how well intentioned, is optional and conditional…the teacher, the school principal, the coach, the aunt and uncle. Consequently the relationships your child builds through such arrangements are optional and conditional as well.

Your help and the resulting relationship you build with your child is likely the only help and relationship in your child's early years that has the potential to be primary and unconditional. When you drop the parenting ball, others who want to help, offer to help and try to help, cannot pick up the ball that you dropped. **You cannot be replaced.**

Special-ness

We wanted to convey to our children that they have tremendous value, that there is something extraordinarily special about them. I call this special-ness.

Special-ness is not because of anything the child does or possesses. It is intrinsic to him or her. This special-ness is best conveyed rather quietly with humility and unconditional commitment over many years. It allows for and enables the many instances of parental discipline and correction to be effective as the child grows up and matures.

Children pay attention to who and what they think values them. When a child is on the receiving end of a primary and unconditional commitment from his or her parent that conveys special-ness and value, he or she pays attention! Through a process similar, I suspect, to osmosis, the child comes to understand over time that he or she intrinsically has value. Since children *value what is valued*, he or she begins to take on the personal responsibility of maturing and developing what is special and valuable: him or herself. "I am valued; therefore I will value myself." The child gradually takes on the personal responsibility of building his or her positive and successful future.

Special-ness is an experience that has much greater depth than what is commonly described by phrases such as positive self-image or self-esteem. Special-ness and intrinsic personal value are at the core of the successful child. It is not the result of being told certain things. It is the by-product of a primary and unconditional commitment a parent makes to his or her child over many years and the resulting relationship. This intrinsic value or special-ness is built to last a lifetime and strong enough to withstand countless storms.

Your Relationship: Presence

Being a significant factor in your child's life does not automatically accompany your child's birth certificate. Everything worthwhile must be earned. As you make and follow through on a primary commitment to raising and guiding your child, your relationship with your child is strengthened. Your child sees evidence that you care about his or her well-being. He or she derives a feeling of personal value and special-ness from your unconditional commitment. Increasingly you are viewed by your child as a source of what is useful and correct. None of this happens when you do not exercise your parental authority and defer to others to raise your child either by choice or by default.

Your developing relationship with your child can be likened to a bank account. When you make an unconditional commitment to your relationship with your child and assume a primary responsibility for raising him or her, each day provides numerous opportunities to make significant deposits into the Credibility and Respect (C & R) Account. When you do not consistently meet this commitment, withdrawals from the C & R Account occur. A low balance in that account will limit your ability to teach and influence your child in the future. The greater the balance in that account, the more influence you will have with your child and the more likely you will be your child's first and most important teacher. A high balance in your account creates what I call *Presence*.

Shortly after my father's death, I received a card from a cousin who was very close to our family. In that sympathy card he described my father as having *presence*. What a great adjective to describe him! In the days following, I thought a great deal about that observation. What exactly is *presence*? I have concluded that *Presence* is the sum total of a lot of credibility and respect. My brother and I had great respect for our father. The balance of his Credibility and Respect Account was huge.

Children pay attention to *Presence*. *Presence* is what prompts children to think in a new or unusual situation, "What would Mom or Dad do now?" Or, "What would their advice be on handling this situation?" *Presence* elicits from children a desire to please and honor their parents through their actions. *Presence* inspires. It does not intimidate. *Presence* provides children with clarity, parameters and direction. It is what continues to influence me long after my father's passing even as I move rapidly into grandparenthood and my hair color continues to transition from brown through to grey and onto white.

How does *Presence* happen? I offered my answer to this question in my eulogy at my father's funeral. In describing my father, I suggested that *Presence* is the outcome of a lifetime of decisions he made while working hard to be a successful parent. He wasn't perfect, and he certainly had some flaws, but for him:

- the well-being of his children was a top priority;
- he provided a foundation of consistency and integrity that his children could count on;
- he demonstrated his respect for his children;
- when necessary, he opted for discipline and teaching, not punishment;
- he did what he said he would do; and
- he provided an example of living that was worthy of being replicated.

Presence, the sum total of a lot of credibility and respect, is only possible when a parent assumes and embraces a primary and unconditional responsibility for raising his or her child.

Basic #2

A child earns privileges by successfully assuming responsibilities.

Remember your child as an infant? Do you recall those early days when your child viewed you and everything else solely for his or her use and pleasure? If your child could speak, you would hear: "Feed me." "Play with me." "That's mine." "Pay attention to me."

As your child grows physically and ages, there is no guarantee that his or her self-centered outlook will automatically change. Proof of this is the adults you and I know who see everything as solely for their own use and benefit. Typically, these adults are pretty miserable. They have few, if any, meaningful relationships. Their attitude towards others prevents them from succeeding as well as they might in their work or professions. They are pretty isolated. Your child will maintain this 'me first' outlook from infancy into adulthood and experience similar results unless you teach him or her to do otherwise.

You are in charge of this teaching process. As such, you should be clear about what attitudes and behaviors you will be teaching your child to develop. You should also expect your child to assume age-appropriate responsibilities to contribute to the family well-being. I recall various jobs as a child including dish washing, taking the trash out, making my bed, shoveling, etc. All of this, you will be teaching your child.

By embracing **Basic #2**, you will be teaching with purpose and direction. You will be helping your child learn how to behave appropriately and develop the outlook and skills necessary to become happy, independent, moral and purposeful. All of your guidance, discipline and correction must bear this long-term view in mind. This is very different from the Authoritarian/Dictatorial parenting style which uses edicts and commands with no accompanying explanation for orders that are issued. No teaching takes place with that parenting style because there is no long-term outcome or vision in mind.

In order to successfully teach your child how to respond positively to your expectations and successfully meet these responsibilities, it is important for you to understand the distinction between *responsibilities, privileges* and *entitlements*. I have seen this distinction portrayed in a number of ways but none more succinctly than in the very unusual location of Alcatraz Island in San Francisco Bay.

As today's visitors to Alcatraz disembark the tour boat and walk up onto the Island, it is impossible not to see a prominently placed plaque. This is the same plaque that was viewed by prisoners arriving at Alcatraz for the first time many years ago. It reads:

You are entitled to food, clothing, shelter, and medical attention.

Everything else is a privilege.

Not only was this applicable to Al Capone and the Birdman of Alcatraz years ago. It has long struck me that this is brilliantly applicable to our children today!

So, what do *privileges, responsibilities* and *entitlements* have to do with each other and how should you use these concepts in raising your successful child?

Following are several scenarios that describe their interplay:

Scenario #1:

My wife and I are responsible for providing adequate shelter, food, nutrition and clothing for our children. One could say that our children are *entitled* to these. The *responsibilities* that we expect them to assume at this point in their lives include feeding the pets daily, taking the trash out as needed, washing the dishes alternately with their siblings, doing their best in school and keeping their bedroom habitable. They are not *entitled* to go to the movie theater on Friday night with friends, but we may extend to them the *privilege* of doing so, if they successfully meet their *responsibilities* during the preceding week.

Scenario #2:

A *responsibility* of our children is to treat each family member respectfully. *Privileges* such as television time, computer time or any of the other many privileges to which most children would love access, depend on meeting this *responsibility*. Such activities are not *entitlements*. They are *privileges* that must be earned. If a child is not respectful and therefore does not meet this *responsibility*, then corresponding *privileges* are not earned and will not be extended to him or her.

Scenario #3:

My wife and I are *responsible* for clothing our children. For us, this includes providing sneakers for them to use at home and school. From our perspective, having sneakers is an *entitlement* for each of the kids. As a new school year approaches and our child's old sneakers are worn and starting to be a little too snug to wear, a purchase of new sneakers is in order. Our child is not *entitled* to the most expensive pair on the shelf. However, if he or she wants the more expensive pair and she has met her *responsibilities*, we might strike a deal and allow her the *privilege* of purchasing the more expensive pair. For such a purchase we would pay what we would typically pay and he or she would pay the difference. The child's share might come from funds earned doing odd jobs such as babysitting or gift money received on various occasions.

Scenario #4:

Our *responsibility* is to make sure our children are adequately clothed, fed and attending school. These are *entitlements* for our children. Their *responsibility* is to do their best in all areas of school involvement. With the help of teachers, we developed a pretty good idea about the kinds of grades they are capable of earning. Earning these grades becomes a *responsibility* of our children. Just as with other *responsibilities*, as they are successfully handled, *privilege*s may become available. *Privileges* such as staying at a friend's house, or having a friend visit, going to a movie or some other fun time, depend on their meeting this school *responsibility*.

In each scenario, we parents are the administrators of the process. When you implement this **Basic** in your family, your child gains access to a privilege by meeting his or her responsibilities. What an empowering concept! Think about it. He or she can enjoy whatever great privileges and opportunities that you and your child agree upon, so long as he or she earns them by meeting certain defined responsibilities. For your child, the sky is the limit! You are simply setting up the expectations and following through on making sure your child experiences the consequences of his or her behavior and attitudes.

Your child earns whatever consequences--good or bad--that you hand out. This needs to be understood very clearly by your child. You will likely need to highlight this concept for your child repeatedly over time because that is how children learn this vital insight. *Your child is responsible for the consequences of his or her behavior. You are simply the administrator!* When privileges are earned because responsibilities are met or exceeded, your child can enjoy both the earned privilege and a great sense of accomplishment. When privileges are not earned and enjoyed, it is not your fault. Your child has simply opted not to meet his or her responsibilities and enjoys (or not) the results of his or her choices.

When a child does not meet his or her responsibilities and does not earn a particular privilege, it is not unusual for that child to be upset or sad. The particularly skillful and manipulative child will try to blame his or her parent for the unpleasant outcome. When a parent capitulates because of the child's sadness, that parent is stealing from his or her child an opportunity to learn one of life's most important lessons! *Don't do it!* Remember, your child earned whatever consequences come his or her way. Children need to understand the connections between *entitlements, responsibilities* and *privileges*. It is one of the most significant lessons required for building a successful life.

I think many of today's parents are very confused about what their child is entitled to and what their child should earn as a privilege. Don't be! This confusion sometimes results from how other parents handle their parental responsibilities. Parents don't always agree on what an entitlement is and what a privilege is. Sometimes this comes in the form of your child saying, "The other kids are able to do that. Why can't I?"

The Alcatraz plaque was so striking to me when I first saw it because it clearly delineates the difference between entitlements and privileges and offers a good perspective for parents on how to define the two terms. The truth is that there really are very few entitlements. I think that many of what today's parents consider to be entitlements are, upon more careful scrutiny, really privileges to be earned. When these two are confused everyone loses.

No one can teach your children this very important connection better than you!

Excellence and Mediocrity

As your child learns the value of meeting his or her responsibilities, it is important that he or she understands the difference between *Excellence* and *Mediocrity*. Wise teacher and coach, John Wooden observed, "Do not try to be better than someone else but make every effort to become the very best you can be." You want to teach your child to handle his or her responsibilities and to do so with excellence, being the very best he or she can be. If something is worth doing, it is worth doing well.

As I was growing up, my brother and I had the task of putting the garbage pails at the curb on Wednesday nights for the Thursday morning pick-up. Taking the garbage out in a mediocre way included: forgetting to do the job and having to be reminded by my mother; complaining about having to do it; leaving the top of the garbage pail on the ground after it fell off which allowed the neighborhood dogs to create quite a mess during the night. Excelling at taking the garbage included: realizing it was Wednesday night and undertaking the task without reminders; making sure that all trash from within the house was emptied into the garbage pail before taking it to the curb; making sure the top of the garbage pail was secure when it was left at the curb.

As your child successfully handles responsibilities with excellence, he or she needs to be reminded of the significance of what is being mastered. Handling responsibilities with excellence is a significant key to succeeding at life. As he or she is earning privileges by meeting responsibilities with excellence at the age of 7 or 8, he or she is mastering a pattern of earning privileges by meeting responsibilities with excellence that can be used at the ages of 17 or 18, and 57 or 58.

Basic #3

A parent's example serves as a very influential model for a child to follow.

The apple doesn't fall far from the tree.

Which of the parents do you think she looks like?

You walk just like your father with the way your hands hang at your side.

I am a fan of the American artist, Norman Rockwell. During a tour of the Rockwell museum, I learned that this great American artist had the habit of sketching what he wanted his paintings to look like before he took to the canvas. One of my favorite Rockwell paintings portrays Rockwell painting himself as he looks at himself in a mirror. Sure enough, there in the painting was the sketch. At the risk of oversimplifying the artist's methods, Rockwell would continuously look at the sketch as he painted his masterpiece.

So what do Rockwell's painting habits have to do with being a successful parent? We are the sketch, or the image, that our children constantly view in order to build their lives. Is the 'sketch' which is represented by your attitudes and actions, substance from which your child can build a 'masterpiece' of a life?

In my professional work long ago, I met a young boy who had run away from home in response to a difficult situation. I arranged to have a meeting with the young man and his parents in hopes of working out some kind of reconciliation. As the four of us spoke, a recent occurrence was described that was very instructive. Apparently, the father and mother had been having a disagreement over some matter. The father's voice grew louder, and the mother apparently met him decibel for decibel.

Shortly afterwards, the father stormed out of the house and remained away for several hours. As we discussed this event, the father disclosed that his leaving of the home was not at all unusual when there was disagreement or tension in the home. I then asked if there were any similarities between the child running away and the father's departure from the home when things get difficult. There was silence as the father connected the dots. He realized that in discussing his son's behavior, he was also discussing and describing his own. He recognized that his son was simply replicating his own example of how to solve a difficult problem. Father and son reconciled that evening, but I am not sure how long the reconciliation lasted.

How is your painting coming?

Consider your strengths and weaknesses as a person and parent. What are your assets? Liabilities? Your child knows what they are. He or she may not be able to describe them precisely, but you are being watched and observed daily. Few things are missed. Your child is learning from your behaviors and attitudes every day and adopting much of what he or she sees.

Our children so want to believe in us parents. They want us to succeed. I have marveled at how a child can see serious inconsistencies between what his or her parent says and does and still feel warmly towards that parent. They don't expect us to be perfect, but they are tremendously inspired and empowered watching us work to improve in some aspect of living. I am in awe at how patient and forgiving most children can be.

But there comes a tipping point, when a child finally has had enough of what he or she detects as a difference between what a parent says and what that parent does. It is as if there is a quota as to how much hypocrisy can be tolerated. The patience and forgiving give way to small traces of cynicism and distrust that begin to grow.

Cynicism is powerfully negative and destructive. It can be more destructive than poverty, health problems and, frankly, most other conditions that people deplore. With it, a smiling, bubbly and enthusiastic five-year-old evolves into a callous, stern and wary adolescent. The cynical distrust and lack of respect that a child directs at his or her parent often generalizes towards other adults and persons of authority or responsibility. For such a child, the future is not something to be pursued with hopeful enthusiasm and creativity. Rather, the future becomes something to survive, watching behind one's back and using others as he or she has been used and misled.

A good rule of thumb is to imagine at every point that your child is watching you and that what you say and do, your child may likely replicate. Children don't care if we aren't the best parents in the world. They just want us to be the best parents we can be. Most always that will suffice.

Be the sketch from which your child can create a masterpiece.

Basic #4

A consistent, predictable environment allows a child to better understand the predictable structure of adult life.

The phrase, "thinking out of the box," is used to describe problem solving strategies that are unusually inventive and creative. The phrase refers to a puzzle of nine dots arranged in three parallel lines of three dots. Together, they comprise the shape of a square. The challenge is to use four straight lines to connect all nine dots without lifting the pencil from the paper.

I remember first seeing this puzzle and struggling unsuccessfully to solve it. Any solution I would try always involved keeping the four lines within the perimeter, or box, of the nine dots. After giving up and admitting failure, I learned that the successful solution requires drawing several of the four lines outside of the perimeter of the nine dots...hence, "thinking out of the box." "Out of the box thinking" is synonymous with successful, creative and innovative thinking.

I have long thought that a phrase that describes the successful raising of children would be, conversely, "in the box parenting." Let me explain. As a bright, enthusiastic, and recently hired professional with a master's degree newly in hand, I found myself spending a lot of time with children who were having difficulty behaving appropriately at home and in school. In fact, all of these children struggled so badly that they had been forced to leave their homes to live in a supervised residential program. Each young person was trying to learn what he or she needed in order to return to living at home.

There was much that was unique about each of the kids. Most striking, however, was what they all had in common. They all shared a lack of consistent structure as they were growing up. They shared the experience of having few things upon which they could consistently count. One day there were rules while on another day the rules were either changed or absent. On still another day, the rules were present but inconsistently enforced. They could not count on parents being where they said they would be when they said they would or following through on commitments that they had made previously. Every day was different because nothing was predictable.

In an effort to demand structure and predictability, each child in his or her own way would push and push until some authority would push back. Most often the push back was not from a parent but a school principal, a police chief or a family court judge.

"In the box parenting" understands that your child desperately needs predictability and consistency in his or her life. When your child is certain of the boundaries and expectations you provide, he or she won't waste mental energy worrying about them. You as parent will experience only the occasional push back from your child that is more growing pains than anything else. Children need to know that the sun is coming up in the morning and that his or her parents are predictably doing and being today as they were yesterday and will be tomorrow. Not worrying about such matters frees up your child to think about improving from the honor roll to the high honor roll this quarter or running for student council or deciding whether pursuing an engineering career is preferable to a career in medicine. In short, "in the box parenting" provides many of the conditions required for a child to demonstrate "out of the box" success!

When our children were still living at home, I recall our son stopping home on a Saturday evening after some activity at school. He needed to ask about going somewhere or doing something that was not on the agreed-upon agenda. As he came into the house and posed his question, I was struck by the fact that he knew we were going to be home at that point because we told him we would be. Such a simple thing, but it makes all the difference. There was a predictable structure to his everyday life that he didn't have to worry about creating for himself. We provided it for him with our rules, expectations and our following through on them in the same way day after day.

Our expectations and pattern of living were very predictable to our children. Even when schedules were unpredictable and inconsistent, as they were from time to time, our expectations and commitments to them remained predictable and consistent. They came to know what we would say and how we would react to a situation before we did. They could count on it. Because we practiced "in the box parenting" with our children, they could practice "out of the box" success as they launched into their futures. They could be successful, creative and inventive as they built their lives because they didn't have to worry about the foundation and structure upon which their lives were being built.

Following are nine areas of a child's life for which successful parents have clear and predictable expectations for their children. They provide an "in the box" structure.

- Family: Are you meeting your responsibilities to our family? This is a home, not just a place to hang your hat.
- Talents and Abilities: Are you focused on exploring and fully developing your capabilities? Don't worry about being the best. Work at being the best.
- Friendships: Are you associating and building relationships with peers who are uplifting and aspiring?
- Time: Are you utilizing each day to become the best person you can become?
- Purpose: Are you reflecting upon and building a future consistent with your dreams, aspirations and faith?
- Values: Is your daily behavior reflective of our family's values and attitudes?
- Language: Do the words you use honor yourself and our family?

- School: Are you fully utilizing the opportunities provided to you in your schooling?
- Community: How are you contributing to the well-being of our community?

With these areas of expectation in mind, then, following are a few of the many questions that are very reasonable for successful parents to ask their children:

- Where is it that you said you would like to go and when is it that you would like to be home? (With no guarantees that either will be acceptable!)

- With whom are you going to be spending time?

- Is all of your homework done and can I see it?

- When is Open House for School? I want to meet your teachers.

- Are all of your chores done? If they aren't you will not be able to go to the movies.

- What sports and activities are you becoming involved with this year?

- I think you have been playing with that video game enough. Please go outdoors and rake the lawn or pick up your fun book and read a chapter.

- What is your report card goal for this marking period?

- Who are your best friends in school this year? I would like to meet their parents.

- What book are you reading now?

- What goals are you working on this month?

All of these questions, and many, many more, are common sense and reasonable questions for you to ask your child. They are also questions for which your child should have ready and acceptable answers. In asking and then getting acceptable answers to these questions and others, you are providing a structure of expectations within which your child can grow and thrive.

By providing this structure of expectations, you will teach your child several lessons. First, your child will learn what is important from what you consider to be important. Second, your child will know of your care and concern more than any utterance can provide. In the game of raising successful children, your child is asking you to "Show me the Structure!" When you provide it day after day, your child learns that he or she can count on you no matter what.

Isn't it ironic that "in the box" parenting sows the seeds for your child's "out of the box" success? Providing an external structure of consistent expectations and discipline for your child helps him or her develop internal self-discipline, self-reliance and direction.

Basic #5:

A parent's dreams for his or her child's future are very influential in the child's life.

What is your hope quotient? Do you have a high hope quotient, a medium hope quotient or a low hope quotient?

Dr. C. Richard Snyder defines hope as goal-oriented thinking. Hope, according to Snyder, first involves aspiring and identifying desirable dreams and goals. (See acknowledgments at the end of the book.) It also includes the pursuit and problem solving involved with accomplishing those goals and dreams. Finally, hope includes the pushing through and persistence required in order to make those goals or dreams come true. A person's hope quotient is a measure of the degree to which a person demonstrates these three elements of goal-oriented thinking.

The higher your hope quotient, the more you are motivated and influenced by your own dreams and goals. A low hope quotient suggests that you, for whatever reason, are not concerned about dreams and goals. Maybe you think that pursuing dreams is childish, that your best days have already happened. Or, you think that dreams aside, your future is really determined by luck or fate. You think that no matter your effort or intent, your future is what is handed to you by forces out of your control.

Snyder tells us that children with high hope quotients, in other words, children who think about and pursue dreams and goals, typically do better in school, have more friends and wisely stay clear of negative risk-taking activities. The higher your child's hope quotient, the more successful and happy he or she will be.

Your hope quotient has a lot to do with your child's because children often reflect the outlook of their parents. Does your child's hope quotient match yours? Knowing now the importance of your child's hope quotient, would you be pleased or concerned if it did match yours?

Building Your Child's Hope Quotient

In the movie *Titanic*, there is a moment when Rose, played by Kate Winslet, realizes why she is so taken with the character, Jack, played by Leonardo DiCaprio. Rose says to Jack, "You see people." What she is referring to is Jack's ability to *see* her with all of her talents, abilities and possibilities. An important part of this kind of *seeing* is that Jack also conveyed to her what those possibilities might be. As Jack does this, Rose becomes inspired and begins to recognize the inadequacy of the arranged marriage being planned for her. She begins to aspire for more. Her hope quotient goes up. *Jack sees Rose not solely as she is but as she can be and conveys this observation to her.*

Think of an adult in your life who stands out as someone who has impacted you in a very positive and special way. For me, a former teacher and coach comes to mind. Well into my adulthood, I loved seeing Coach Borgognoni. I first met Coach when I was in middle school. He was my physical education teacher and also coached me in several sports during high school. During those years he did what most teachers and coaches do. In some situations, he would talk normally while at other times, the decibels got a little louder. But, he was always teaching. And, through it all, he always made me feel special. I left every interaction with him with more of a bounce in my step.

I have thought about Coach Borgognoni often through the years. What is it that he did that so influenced my relationship with him? He always saw me as I could be, or at least I felt that he did. He didn't just see me with my shortcomings and failings.

He recognized my strengths. He saw what I was capable of being and doing and he conveyed this to me by how he treated me and what he said to me. As a result, I became more mindful of my strengths and abilities. He wanted me to succeed so much that I came to want to succeed. To use Rose's vernacular, "He *saw* me." He raised my personal hope quotient and because he and several others did the same, I am better for it.

How do you *see* your child? Do you *see* him or her in terms of shortcomings alone? Or, do you *see* the wonderful unfolding mystery taking place as your child learns about his or her talents and abilities that are calling out to be developed?

And, do you convey what you *see* to your child? I am not suggesting that you puff your child's ego up with unrealistic and sappy plaudits. That is not helpful. But, I do know that all children are extraordinarily special and that all children have talents and abilities, however varied they may be. Are you *seeing* these and conveying this perspective to your child? If you are, you are positively impacting your child's hope quotient. Great work!

Be Aware = Beware

You have to be very careful and aware as you seek to positively impact your child's aspirations and dreams. As you communicate with your child, are you mindful of focusing on *his* or *her* dreams, goals and strengths? Or, do you see your child as a means for you to finally reach your own long delayed dreams and goals? Doing the former is a significant contribution to helping your child build a successful life. Doing the other will diminish your child's future and your relationship with him or her. This is a very important question for a parent to consider. It is equally important that in answering the question you pay strict attention to the 11th Commandment: Don't fake yourself out!

I recently spoke with a former teacher of mine. During his college career, Vince was a tremendous baseball pitcher and, after many years, still holds numerous pitching records at his alma mater. I asked him about his family and he began speaking proudly about one of his son's very successful musical performances during his college career. Vince was as excited about his son's musical performances as he would have been with a no-hitter in baseball. After helping his son grow, discover and develop his own talents and strengths, Vince was describing the thrill and excitement of watching his child make his own unique dreams and goals come true.

Our youngest child struggled to discover what have turned out to be some of her tremendous strengths and talents. She was a good student in high school and had an opportunity before graduating to do an internship in the business office of a local company. She did well, enjoyed the people and thought she might want to prepare for a career in accounting. She applied to and was accepted at a university with a strong business school. She began her college career and it was as if she ran into a wall at 60 mph. Macroeconomics. Microeconomics. Accounting. Ouch!!

It didn't take long before she and we realized that she needed to make a mid-course correction. As she thought through her options, she observed what should have been so obvious. She has an unusually gifted capacity to help young people. Kids are attracted to her as iron filings are to a magnet. It is not something she works at but rather, it just happens. And, she enjoys helping them. The more difficult and challenging the kid, it seems, the better. Perhaps, she and we thought, she could utilize and develop this strength in the field of teaching. With the mid-course correction into the field of education, she built a tremendous college record. She is successfully embarking on a career path that builds on her strengths and talents.

As parents trying to assist and support our daughter through this difficult experience, we tried to keep our focus on helping her discover her strengths and talents and then, helping her figure out how best to develop them. This outlook served her and us well as we watched her grow, mature and succeed. She came to see herself with exciting potential and capabilities and acted on them. The temporary bump in the road really didn't matter. Today, she is well on her way to making a number of her dreams and goals come true.

An effective parent focuses on helping his or her child's dreams come true, not on helping a child make the parent's dreams come true.

Basic #6:

A lot of quality time is required to raise a successful child.

For years I have heard the debate about what amount of time parents need to invest in raising a child successfully. The debate has intensified through the years as a growing number of two parent families opt for two income producers and single parents feel the financial pressures daily. Do children require "quality" time or "quantity" time? Or, put another way, how much quality time is needed? The successful parent knows when enough is enough and understands that the answer is not a simple math equation.

Our oldest child was starting her first job after college on the other side of the continent and she asked my wife and me to accompany her to check out the area. In preparing for the week-long trip, our other two children who stayed home were instructed on how to take care of the plants and flowers at our home. Directions on watering and the required frequency were clearly outlined.

We went on our trip, checked things out and returned home a week later. As we drove into our driveway, we saw that the plants and flowers were beyond reach. There was no saving them. It was clear that our directions were not followed and that they had not been cared for. When we asked our two other children about the situation, they told us that their schedules were just too hectic and busy to do the watering job as it had been outlined to them…unbelievable. Were we being given an excuse or a legitimate and justifiable explanation? It really didn't matter. The plants and flowers still required watering.

Kids are a lot like those plants and flowers. A parent's

rationale for how he or she allocates time to parenting does not diminish the child's needs. They are what they are. If your child's needs are successfully met, good things happen. If your child's needs are not successfully met, it doesn't matter if your rationale is an excuse or a legitimate explanation. Your child's needs and development are negatively impacted.

Following Through

If you are going to have expectations for your child's behavior and he or she does not comply with those expectations, you must respond in a timely manner. If your child does not meet a particular expectation, there must be an immediate consequence to the behavior. Remember the discussion about entitlements, privileges and responsibilities?

When you do not follow through on your expectations in a timely manner, you are conveying several messages, none of which are helpful, to your child:

- Your child quickly finds out that your expectations for acceptable behaviors and attitudes don't really matter to you and therefore he or she will not honor them.

- Your actions do not match up at all with what you are verbally requesting. You are planting seeds of hypocrisy and cynicism for your child to harvest.

- You are conveying a lack of care and concern to your child. Children understand that parents attend to what they value. When a parent does not attend with consistency to following through on the structure that has been set up, the child concludes that he or she is not really valued.

Relationship Building

It takes time to know your child.

Our middle child has taken on a number of significant and life-threatening challenges in his life. I marvel at his courage and thoughtful daring. But, on a quiet evening at home we learned about something that used to stop him in his tracks immediately. Point the television remote at him and everything comes to a halt. A typically self-assured, confident and adventurous teenage soul, he would almost wilt as he worried about the harm that could befall him from the television remote being pointed at him. It was hilarious. It takes time spent with your child to know your child, quirks and all.

A mother's intuition about the well-being of her child is something I would never question or dispute. I recall years ago our three-year-old climbing out of her bed and scampering into our bedroom and up onto our bed. Her disposition seemed a little off and she felt somewhat warm. Should we arrange to visit her doctor or wait it out? Our decision—really, my wife's decision—was to visit the doctor only to find that our daughter was diagnosed with scarlatina, a precursor to scarlet fever. It was vital that she was seen by our doctor. Mother's intuition? Or, was the decision made because my wife knew her child well enough to know to make the correct decision. It takes time spent with your child to know your child. There is no short cut to getting to know your child.

A parent's calendar is a reflection of what he or she values. A child learns much from where he or she fits into the parent's calendar.

For the parent who has invested him or herself into the life of a child and *Presence* has been established, the limits of time can be somewhat overcome. Such a parent can still be somewhat present to his or her child without being in close proximity to that child. I think of the naval officer who commanded a submarine and would be deployed for 3 to 6 months at a time. Because of how he and his wife parented their children, he was very much present to his son and daughter even when underwater!

However, in most instances, a parent's time constraints, whether they are real or imagined, matter a great deal when it comes to raising a successful child and must be overcome. Remember, in this respect, children are a lot like plants and flowers!

So, how much quality time is required to raise a successful child? My answer is, you have invested a sufficient amount of quality time when you have successfully:

- Implemented and followed through on your expectations for your child;

- Come to know your child well;

- Built a relationship with your child that he or she considers affirming and supportive; and

- Developed Presence with your child.

My wife and I are now on the other end of the child rearing task, enjoying wonderful friendships with our adult children and the thrill of spending time with terrific grandchildren. Knowing what I know now, I can't imagine anything so important and valuable that would be worth short cutting the time required to successfully raise our children.

Basic #7

A child's dignity and personal worth are derived largely from his or her relationship with the parent(s).

Your child does not need you to be his or her friend in order to become a happy, independent, moral and purposeful adult. Your child needs you to be his or her parent. This is at odds with what a parent who utilizes the Permissive Parenting Style often says: "I just want to be a friend to my child."

We all want our children to be confident and feel valued. Parents who embrace the Permissive Parenting Style place a high priority on providing warm and fuzzy experiences and interactions for and with their children. However, they avoid exercising their parental authority for fear of threatening their parent-child relationship or creating situations for their children that can be difficult, discouraging and disappointing. The warm and fuzzy times are certainly pleasant and enjoyable. But, the positive outcomes that the Permissive Parent hopes for from these moments are fleeting at best

The effective parent understands that there is more to providing a foundation of dignity and self-worth for his or her child than warm and fuzzy. In spite of, and often because of exercising parental authority he or she knows that there are multiple ways to provide a child with a solid foundation of personal dignity and self- worth for a lifetime. Warm and fuzzy has its limits.

We wanted our children to understand clearly that our concern, support and love were nothing that could be earned. Let me repeat that. *We wanted our children to understand clearly that our concern, support and love were nothing that could be earned.*

We wanted them to know that our commitment to their well-being was unconditional. It did not depend on good school grades, though we expected them to do their best in school. It did not depend on appearance or behavior, though we expected them to be polite and respectful always. We did not barter with our concern, support and love. We were unconditionally committed to them.

I enjoy listening to our adult children share stories with us about their young children. There is a real joy in their voices. Certainly they get tired and frustrated on occasion. But they enjoy watching their special little children grow, change and develop. What a thrill! It is evident in their descriptions, in the stories they share and in the looks in their eyes. These kids are remarkably special to them.

That special-ness cannot be earned. It is wrapped up in the remarkable little children that they are. I am sure that you know what I am writing about as you think of your own child. It is that special-ness, that awe that you feel when you stand back and gaze at your child that you need to convey to your child. This is what provides your child with that foundation of personal dignity and worth you want for him or her. *Providing this is not at odds with exercising your parental authority when required.*

Conveying Special-ness

When considering ways to convey special-ness to their child, most parents immediately think in terms of telling their child about that special-ness. Doing so is very important. I recall making it a point as often as I could to help put our children to bed at night. Typically, a story was read, and prayers said. Then there was a golden opportunity for a short but powerful conversation. I borrowed from a favorite writer of mine, Denis Waitley, a way to communicate this special-ness in a unique but powerful way. I would tell each child how proud I was to share the same last name with him or her. I was proud to be their parent.

Another way that I tried to convey that special-ness was in an annual Christmas letter to each of the children. This practice extended well into their adulthood. I found such letters to be great opportunities to discuss triumphs from the previous year and excitement for adventures in the upcoming year. More importantly, they provided me opportunities to tell each child how special he or she is to my wife and me. Various gestures over the years have reaffirmed to me how effective those letters were at conveying that special-ness to our children. Similar efforts could be effective at other times such as birthdays or the beginning and end of a school year.

But, *words can do only so much*. We have high expectations for what we value. If you want your child to feel valued, then expect a great deal from him or her. Expect your child to be his or her best. Anything less is not compatible with the special-ness you see in him or her. The focus is not on your child being the best, but rather on being his or her best. Furthermore, since you are committed to helping your child be his or her personal best, then develop a predictable and consistent structure of expectations and routines within which your child will grow and thrive. And then follow through with implementing that set of expectations and routines. That is when the excitement begins!

Conveying Special-ness When Your Child Is Not Acting Very Special!

It is easy to care about and be committed to a loveable child. But, what happens when your child does not comply with your expectations and routines? In fact, what happens when your special, loveable child disappears and leaves behind a difficult, challenging kid who is hardly recognizable? This is a crucial time for you to parent. It is also an opportunity--to teach, change behaviors and convey special-ness!

If your relationship with your child is that of a friend relating to a friend, you might seriously consider throwing your hands up and walking away at a time like this. Remember, though, you are not your child's friend. You are your child's parent. When your child is not behaving in a loveable manner, you must be committed to your child's well-being no matter what. Your commitment is not earned. It is without condition. By following through with whatever consequences are appropriate, you tenaciously demonstrate to your child just how special and valuable he or she is. Even if your child is not acting in ways that lead to building a successful life, you have enough desire for the two of you. As you follow through on what you have to do to successfully parent your child, he or she will learn to develop the attitudes and behaviors you expect. In doing so, you will also have conveyed to your child how special he or she is!

The parent who uses the Permissive Parenting Style tries to avoid holding his or her child accountable to a consistent structure of expectations and routines for fear of negatively impacting the parent-child relationship. This approach does a disservice to the child in several ways. First, the child does not learn appropriate behaviors and the importance of being accountable to important adults. Second, it is a lost relationship building opportunity between parent and child.

Parents need to be reassured that a significant and powerful way to convey value to their children is to hold them accountable to a consistent structure of expectations and routines. Few people I know enjoy confrontations. Often such times are unpleasant and uncomfortable. But, it is at times like these when you hold your child accountable, that your relationship will ultimately be strengthened, not weakened.

Any parent can talk with his or her child about love, care and concern when things are going great. But, children are very smart. They see through the shallowness and limited value of such words when this is a parent's sole strategy for conveying special-ness. They recognize and value commitment and concern when they see it demonstrated day after day through a parent's actions. When you embrace and exercise your parental authority in the ways described, be assured that your child will walk into the future behaving in an appropriate manner with dignity and personal worth. And, you and your child will share a strong, affirming relationship

Basic #8

Teaching a child a faith-based orientation to life is vital.

This Basic is not meant to evangelize or proselytize. Rather, it is rooted in a growing body of formidable secular research that observes strongly that children need to consider and connect to matters of ultimate importance such as purpose and faith. How you provide for this Basic is up to you, but to ignore it is akin to ignoring gravity. Following are three examples of the secular research to which I refer.

National Study of Youth and Religion

The *National Study of Youth and Religion* is a research project directed by Christian Smith, Professor in the Department of Sociology at the University of Notre Dame and Lisa Pearce, Assistant Professor of Sociology at the University of North Carolina at Chapel Hill. Beginning in 2001 as the largest study of its kind, the research project continued through 2015. The purpose of the study was to learn about the influence of religion and spirituality in the lives of American young people in order to foster an informed national discussion about this topic.

Parents should be very encouraged as the research points out that most children look to their parents for guidance on this and other matters. Children are significantly influenced by their parents with respect to religion and spirituality. Following are highlights of the various sections of the completed research:

> ▪ Teens in religiously involved families tend to report that their parents have stronger relationships than teens in families not religiously involved.

- Teens in religiously involved families tend to have stronger family relationships than teens in families not religiously involved.

- Family religious activity including parental attendance and parental prayer are significantly associated with positive family relationships.

- Religious U.S. 12th graders hold more positive attitudes about life than their less-religious peers. These positive attitudes include:

  - positive attitudes towards themselves,

  - feeling like their lives are useful,

  - feeling hopeful about their future,

  - feeling like life is meaningful, and

  - enjoying being in school.

- Children involved with religious activities are less likely to participate in many delinquent and risky behaviors.

Hardwired to Connect

Hardwired to Connect: The New Scientific Case for Authoritative Communities was written by The Commission on Children at Risk and published in 2003. The Commission was an independent, jointly sponsored initiative of YMCA of the USA, Dartmouth Medical School and the Institute for American Values. Its principal investigator was Dr. Kathleen Kovner Kline of Dartmouth Medical School. The Commission was comprised of 33 children's doctors, research scientists and mental health and youth service professionals. It was a very diverse and highly regarded group, including such notables as T. Berry Brazelton, Robert Coles, James P. Comer, Thomas Insel, Kathleen Kovner Kline and Alvin Poussaint. Its mission was to investigate empirically the social, moral and spiritual foundations of child well-being, to evaluate the degree to which current practice and policy in the U.S. recognize those foundations, and to make recommendations for the future.

The Commission examined the growing emotional and behavioral problems of U.S. children which continue to challenge the capacity of the nation's mental health system. These concerns about young people included high and rising rates of depression, anxiety, attention deficit, conduct disorders, thoughts of suicide and other serious mental, emotional, and behavioral problems.

The Commission made numerous observations that are relevant to you successfully raising your child. Drawn from the newest and most authoritative science about child development, the Commission noted that your child is *hardwired to connect!* That is, from the fields of neuroscience and behavioral science, your child's make up is such that he or she needs to build positive and meaningful relationships with other people: *Connect to people!* Further, your child is also *hardwired to connect*, or needs to find a *meaningful understanding of matters relating to moral meaning, purpose and spirituality*: *Connect to purpose!* The Commission observed that when a child's need to connect in these two ways is stifled or blocked, he or she begins to experience behavioral and emotional difficulty.

The Commission also sees the Family Unit as the most effective means by which children can learn about connecting to People and Purpose. The Commission recommends that one of the most important priorities for parents to be successful parents is the *encouragement of their child's spiritual and religious development.*

Dr. James Garbarino

Shortly after I read his book, *Lost Boys: Why Our Sons Turn Violent and How We Can Save Them*, I was able to hear Dr. James Garbarino speak at a regional meeting of the American Psychological Association (APA). I heard some things I am not used to hearing at academic presentations! Let me explain.

Garbarino is a noted psychologist and author. A major part of his work for the past several decades has focused on young boys who severely hurt, and in some instances, kill others. He was involved in the aftermath of the Columbine killings, interviewing both killers and their parents. I was not surprised when a column he wrote appeared after the Newtown killings. (http://www.cnn.com/2012/12/19/opinion/garbarino-violence-boys/index.html)

Dr. Garbarino has been an expert witness in several of the more well-known and horrendous school killings trials. One of the characteristics he uses to describe young people who are so harmful to others is an absence of a future orientation while at the same time also living in a spiritual vacuum. They do not, says Garbarino, have "spiritual anchors." They experience a crisis of meaninglessness captured best by the slogan, "I am born; I live; I die."

What was surprising to me is that I did not expect to attend an academic APA presentation and hear the guest speaker talk about the important role that spiritual anchors have in giving young people meaning and a sense of purpose and direction. After all, he is not a pastor, minister or priest and the setting did not call for a sermon or homily! For me, this fact underscores even more the importance of what he is saying about the needs of young people. And, he echoes the work of the National Study of Youth and Religion as well as the Commission on Children at Risk.

A logical conclusion a parent can deduce from all three sources is that an important aspect of raising a successful child is helping your child develop a faith-based orientation or outlook. It is my judgement that doing so involves consistent and regular involvement with a religiously-based institution with which you are comfortable. This will aid you in supporting your child's engagement in a process of reflection about the significant questions of life: Who am I? For what purpose? Towards what end? These are the questions that when considered with guidance and support will help him or her develop those spiritual anchors about which Garbarino writes. How you do this and the shape, size and color of your approach is your call.

Basic #9

A primary task of a parent is taking the mystery out of being successful for the child.

Each spring it happens at least once. A baby robin ends up a little prematurely on the ground and our cat starts drooling and getting ready to have some fun, only to be denied the opportunity as my wife bolts to the young bird's rescue. Watching this drama, I am always reminded how short the growing up period is for a robin and how much longer the growing up period is for children.

Most children, unless taught, do not understand how life works and how to build successful futures. For many young people, all of this is wrapped in a cloak of mystery and uncertainty. It is as if they are proceeding into their futures with blindfolds. It is a parent's task to untie the blindfold and point the way forward.

Basics #1-8 provide a frame of reference for you to use to create your family culture and help you accomplish several goals. First, your child will develop an internal desire to mature and be his or her personal best. Second, your child will acquire a disposition to learn and come to value you as a source of guidance and direction. With this family culture in place, you will be able to successfully handle **Basic #9: A primary task of a parent is taking the mystery out of being successful for the child.**

Being your child's most important teacher will involve sharing lessons you have learned about living and building a successful life with your child. For some parents this is very easy to do. They may have had many conversations with their parents or grandparents that they found to be very valuable. They are able to use their parents and grandparents as role models as they teach their own children. For some parents, however, talking with their children in such a way is foreign and very awkward-- even intimidating.

We want to help and support you in applying **Basic #9: taking the mystery out of being successful for your child**. Our follow-up book with the tentative title, *Helping Your Child Be Goal-Oriented, Purposeful and Positively Motivated* will:

- Share with you the *Nine Winning Practices* which is a framework you can use to teach your child how to build a successful future.

- Empower you to use the culture and the countless teaching opportunities it provides rather than being at the mercy of that culture.

- Help you engage your child in developing goal oriented and purposeful thinking.

Thank you for accepting the challenge to be your child's first and most important teacher. Thank you for doing what is required to earn the credibility and respect from your child that will enable you to successfully meet that challenge.

Your commitment to taking on this most important responsibility is vital. Your child needs you to. We need you to.

Acknowledgments

Diana Baumrind is a developmental psychologist well known for her research on parenting styles. Her work is very helpful in understanding how to be your child's most important teacher. References for Baumrind's work are many. Several helpful ones are:

https://www.parentingforbrain.com/4-baumrind-parenting-styles/

http://www.devpsy.org/teaching/parent/baumrind_parenting_s tyles.pdf

http://psycnet.apa.org/record/1967-05780-001

https://www.livestrong.com/article/1001090-baumrind-theory-parenting-styles/

http://selfdeterminationtheory.org/SDT/documents/2009_Turne rChandleretal_JCSD.pdf

C. Richard Snyder, Ph.D. was a psychology professor who explored extensively various aspects of Positive Psychology. Of particular interest to becoming your child's most important teacher is his work on Hope, goal-oriented thinking. A profile of Dr. Snyder, his research and books are delineated at this link:

http://c.r.snyder.socialpsychology.org/

   Thank you as well to the many people who have assisted throughout the editing process. At the risk of leaving out someone, sincere appreciation is extended to Chris Ramsdell, Diane Barlowe, Shirley Montalbano Walker, Dan Jacobs, Austin LaBarge, Angela Matthews, Cindy and Dan Sgroi, Ray Holz and Bella Bikowski. And, then there is Full Quiver Publishing and the tremendous assistance, guidance and help from Ellen Gable Hrkach and husband, James Hrkach. Thank you.

Last, appreciation is expressed to my immediate family. The original cover format that is being used for all books in the Raising Successful Children Series was created by daughter Tara's husband, Bob Canaway. Son, Tim, read the first manuscript a few years ago and gave tremendous feedback. One book became three books. All three children made raising children a tremendously joyful and meaningful adventure, resulting in my thinking about, studying and discussing this topic for decades. Special thanks go to my wife Mary Jo who has patiently walked with much insight and wisdom through every step of this project with me. Thank you.

If you would like to access more resources for Raising Successful Children, you are invited to register at **www.robertpnewberry.com** for the free, quarterly **Steering Wheel Conversations Newsletter**. Upon your registering, we will send you a PDF of our professionally designed poster outlining **The Basics**.

About the Author

Robert P. Newberry has built a professional legacy of excellence as an educator, counselor and therapist with multiple populations, settings and circumstances ranging from rural and urban upstate New York, to at-risk students in south Texas and teens of deployed National Guardsmen in New Hampshire. In doing this, he has:

- Developed pioneering programming that helps young people from rural and urban areas achieve and excel in spite of personal loss, adversity, and challenges;
- Lectured for regional, state and national professional conferences, and public and private organizations on various themes relating to helping young people become resilient achievers and pursuers of excellence;
- Authored publications for parents and educators regarding raising and educating successful children. These include a subscription and web based bi-weekly column for educators and monthly column for parents which was the basis of the original *Green Beans and Legacies*.

Robert P. Newberry claims, however, that his most important accomplishment is being married to his wife, Mary Jo, for 45 years and together raising three great adult children who have enabled them to be grateful and enthusiastic grandparents of 10 tremendous grandchildren.

Find out more about him at his website:
http://www.RobertPNewberry.com